THE ART OF MASTERING SALES

Vol. 1
Unleashing Your Sales Potential

DEMARIO CROMITY

[Volume 1] Unleashing your Sales Potential [2023]

TABLE OF CONTENTS

Introduction

My Name is Demario Cromity and I have over 20 years of Sales Experience and in that time I've helped several companies generate millions of dollars in revenue, directly and indirectly; through Teaching, Seminars and Training. No matter what industry you are in, you are either selling a product, a service, or your personality. Whether you are a veteran in the field or just starting your career, this book will provide you with the tools, tips, tricks, cheat codes, sales hacks and insights to become an elite salesperson aka the Master. So get ready to learn How to Master the Art of Sales!

Please understand that selling is not just a skill, it is an art form. In this book we will discuss the 3 Es - Energy, Excitement, and Enthusiasm which are crucial ingredients to achieving sales excellence. We will dive into the finer points of building rapport with your prospects, the importance of probing and asking the right questions, and mastering active listening skills. We will also talk about effective bundling, which is combining products or services into packages for the benefit of your client.

You will learn how to sell with confidence, how to position your product or service correctly, and how to effectively close sales using several techniques. We will also explore the art of upselling, and how to counter objections with effective rebuttals.

And last but not least, you will gain a deep understanding of the sales process, learn to achieve your sales goals and become an elite salesperson.

Before we jump into this book I have a few questions: are you ready to unleash your potential, challenge the status quo, and master the strategies that will elevate you to sales greatness??? Are you ready to rewrite the rules, shatter your own limitations, and become the sales champion you were destined to be? The stage is set, the spotlight is on you, and the time for action is now. If you answered yes to all of the questions above, get ready to take your sales game to the next level and master the art of sales.

Chapter 1

The Art of Greetings- Setting the Foundation for Successful Sales

Welcome, sales enthusiasts, to the world of greetings—a fundamental aspect of successful sales interactions. In this Chapter, we'll explore the vital role that greetings play in setting the tone for your sales conversations. Greetings are more than just pleasantries; they are the gateway to building emotional connections with your customers. By mastering the art of greetings, you'll create a positive and engaging environment that enhances your chances of closing sales. Let's dive in and uncover the secrets of impactful greetings!

Section 1: The Power of the First Impression

A warm and genuine greeting serves as the catalyst for a successful sale. Remember, the sale doesn't start when you dive into product details; it begins the moment you greet your customer. Sales, being an emotional game, relies on connecting with customers on a deeper level. By delivering a welcoming greeting, you increase the likelihood of accelerating the sales process. Here are three key points to consider:

Breaking the Ice

A smile, a friendly one-liner, or a genuine compliment can work wonders in breaking the ice. Here are a few examples:

1. I like your shoes. Where did you get those from?
2. Good afternoon. I just wanted you to know that you are a lucky winner and you can purchase any of our products at a regular price today.

These simple gestures help to create a friendly and relaxed atmosphere, allowing customers to let their guard down. Remember, a warm greeting goes beyond words; it's about conveying excitement and genuine interest in serving your customers.

Emotional Engagement:

Customers often make purchasing decisions based on their emotions rather than logical reasoning. Think about it, the better you feel the more likely you are to buy something. Have you ever said I'll get it since you caught me in a good mood? By offering a warm greeting, you create a positive emotional connection with your customers. This sets the stage for a productive sales conversation, where customers feel comfortable and open to exploring your products or services.

The Impact of Positive Experiences:

Consider your own experiences as a customer walking into a business. When you're greeted with warmth and enthusiasm, it leaves a lasting impression. This positive experience fosters trust and a sense of value, making customers more likely to make a purchase, even if they didn't originally plan to do so. On the other side of the coin, a lackluster or absent greeting can immediately turn customers away, leading them to seek out alternative options. Ex: Have you ever visited a store with the intent to purchase a product, didn't receive a warm greeting and decided to leave and purchase the product elsewhere.

Section 2: The Importance of Consistency in Greetings

While first impressions are crucial, consistent greetings are equally vital. Here are three points to remember:

Building Strong Relationships:

Every interaction with a customer presents an opportunity to reinforce a positive relationship. Consistently delivering warm and genuine greetings shows customers that they can expect exceptional service every time they interact with you. This consistency builds trust, loyalty, and increases the chances of repeat business.

Reflecting Professionalism:

Consistent greetings reflect professionalism and a commitment to excellence. When customers know they will always be greeted warmly and respectfully, it creates a positive perception of your business and instills confidence in your products or services. Consistency helps establish you as a reliable and trustworthy salesperson.

Enhancing Brand Image:

Consistent greetings contribute to shaping your brand's image. When customers consistently experience positive interactions and warm greetings, it becomes synonymous with your brand. This positive association helps differentiate your business from competitors and builds a strong reputation in the market.

Section 3: Greetings as a Customer-Centric Approach

An essential aspect of effective greetings is adopting a customer-centric mindset.

Here are a couple points to guide your customer-centric approach:

Personalization:

Tailor your greetings to each individual customer. Pay attention to their preferences, names, and previous interactions. Personalizing greetings shows that you value and remember them as individuals, fostering a deeper connection.

Continual Improvement

Chapter 2

Energize Your Sales- Mastering The Power of Energy, Excitement, and Enthusiasm

Welcome, sales masters, to a transformative tutorial that will electrify your sales transactions! In this exciting journey, we will uncover the secret ingredients of success: Energy, Excitement, and Enthusiasm—collectively known as the 3 Es. Prepare to unleash a tidal wave of positive vibes that will captivate your customers, boost their engagement, and propel your sales to unprecedented heights. Buckle up, as we dive into the realm of high-energy sales!

Section 1: Harnessing the Power of Energy

In this section, we will explore the contagious nature of energy and its profound impact on sales success. Discover how to radiate positive energy that captivates your customers and ignites their interest. Key points to consider:

The Energy Ripple Effect:

1. Energy is a force that transcends words—it's an aura that surrounds you. When you exude high energy, your customers can feel it, and it becomes infectious. As a result, they become more engaged, receptive, and enthusiastic about your product or service. Learn techniques to boost your energy levels and create a vibrant atmosphere that magnetizes customers towards your offerings.

Maintaining Consistent Energy:

2. While bursts of energy are valuable, sustaining energy throughout the entire transaction is crucial. Ensure there are no lulls or moments of disengagement that can dampen the customer's excitement. Learn strategies to maintain a steady flow of positive energy, injecting it into every aspect of your sales conversation, from introductions to demonstrations and closing.

Section 2: Igniting Excitement for Maximum Impact

In this section, we'll explore the art of cultivating excitement and channeling it into sales success. Excitement acts as a catalyst that fuels the customer's interest, amplifying their desire to own your product or service. Here's what you need to know:

Infectious Enthusiasm:

1. When you genuinely exude excitement about your product, customers can sense it. Your passion and belief in what you're offering become contagious, arousing their curiosity and interest. Learn how to effectively convey your excitement through compelling storytelling, highlighting unique features, and showcasing the transformative benefits that await them.

Building Emotional Connections:

2. Excitement has a direct link to emotions. By tapping into your customer's emotions and presenting your product in a way that triggers positive feelings, you establish a deep connection. This emotional bond not only enhances the buying experience but also strengthens the likelihood of a successful sale. Discover techniques to evoke emotions and create memorable experiences that leave customers eager to say "yes."

Section 3: The Power of Enthusiasm- A Continuous Sales Fuel

In this section, we will explore the distinct quality of enthusiasm and its vital role in sales. Enthusiasm is the unwavering passion and dedication that underpins every successful sales transaction. Key points to consider:

Sustaining Emotion:

1. Unlike excitement, which can be spontaneous, enthusiasm requires a degree of intentional activation. It is a well-considered commitment to maintain the emotional connection throughout the entire sales process. Discover techniques to cultivate and preserve enthusiasm, ensuring a consistent and engaging customer experience.

Overcoming Customer Doubts:

2. Maintaining enthusiasm serves as a protective shield against buyer's remorse and second-guessing. By continuously radiating enthusiasm, you create an atmosphere of trust and reassurance. This diminishes doubts and empowers customers to move forward with confidence, confident in their decision to purchase your product or service.

Congratulations, energized sales warriors! You have unlocked the power of the 3 Es—Energy, Excitement, and Enthusiasm—to invigorate your sales transactions. Armed with these powerful tools.

Chapter 3

The Art of Building Rapport - Creating Connections in a Short Time

Welcome, sales enthusiasts, to the world of building rapport! Imagine a world where every sales interaction feels like a conversation with a trusted friend. In this chapter, we will unravel the secrets of building rapport—a crucial skill that paves the way for long-lasting customer relationships. Discover the art of mirroring, the power of the "Me Too" effect, and the hidden nuances that lie within tone, proximity, posture, and gestures. Get ready to create irresistible connections that make your customers feel truly understood and valued.

Section 1: The Power of Rapport in Sales

Building rapport is the cornerstone of successful sales interactions. It sets the stage for open communication, trust, and a positive customer experience. Establishing a connection with your customers not only enhances your likability but also increases the likelihood of a successful sale.

Section 2: Mirroring: Creating Comfort Through Similarity

Mirroring is a technique that involves subtly matching and mirroring the behavior of your customer. This includes mirroring their voice tone, speed, and body language. By doing so, you create a sense of familiarity and comfort, helping to establish a rapport quickly. Be mindful of these mirroring elements:

Voice Tone: Pay attention to the pitch, volume, and overall tone of your customer's voice. Aim to match their tone to create a harmonious conversation.

Voice Speed: Adjust your speaking pace to align with your customer's natural rhythm. If they speak slowly, adopt a slower pace, and vice versa.

Section 3: The "Me Too" Effect: Finding Common Ground

The "me too" effect is a powerful tool for building rapport. It involves finding shared experiences, interests, or perspectives with your customer. By expressing genuine interest and showcasing commonalities, you create a sense of camaraderie and connection. Find opportunities to say "me too" through:

Shared Experiences: Identify shared experiences, such as hobbies, interests, or backgrounds, to establish a common ground. This helps foster a sense of familiarity and shared understanding.

Active Listening: Pay close attention to your customer's stories, experiences, and preferences. Engage in active listening, asking follow-up questions and expressing genuine curiosity. This demonstrates your interest in their world.

Section 4: Non-Verbal Communication: The Silent Language of Rapport

Remember that spoken words only account for 30% of building rapport. The remaining 70% lies in non-verbal cues. Here are essential elements to consider:

Posture: Maintain an open and relaxed posture that conveys approachability. Avoid crossing your arms or displaying defensive body language, as it can create a barrier between you and the customer.

Gestures: Use gestures that mirror the customer's level of expressiveness. If they are animated, feel free to match their level of enthusiasm. However, be mindful of not overpowering or overshadowing their gestures.

Proximity: Be aware of personal space and adjust your distance accordingly. Standing too close can make someone uncomfortable, while standing too far can create a sense of disconnect. Find the right balance that promotes intimacy and comfort.

Eye Contact: Maintain steady eye contact without staring. Show interest and engagement through your gaze while being respectful of cultural differences and personal boundaries.

Section 5: Authenticity: The Key to Lasting Rapport

While techniques are valuable, remember that authenticity is the foundation of building rapport. Be genuinely interested in your customers, approach conversations with sincerity, and create connections based on trust and respect. People can sense when you are being genuine, and it goes a long way in building lasting rapport.

Congratulations, rapport builders! You have discovered the art of establishing meaningful connections in a short time.

Chapter 4

Probing and Questioning - Unlocking the Path to Success

Welcome, aspiring sales experts, to the world of probing! In this chapter, we will delve into the art of asking the right open-ended questions that unveil your customers' deepest desires and motivations. Learn how to navigate conversations with finesse, uncover hidden objections, and identify those powerful buying signs. Get ready to master the art of asking open-ended questions that will guide you towards successful sales interactions!

Section 1: Understanding the Magic of Probing

Probing is the act of asking strategic questions to explore customers' perspectives, uncover their pain points, and understand their motivations. It's like looking through a keyhole to discover the  secret treasures hidden within. By probing, you can gather valuable insights and build stronger connections with your customers.

Section 2: Unleashing the Power of Open-Ended Questions

Open-ended questions are the superhero tools in your probing toolkit. These questions encourage customers to provide detailed answers and share their thoughts, feelings, and experiences. Open-ended questions allow you to dig deeper, gain a deeper understanding, and identify buying signals. Here are five examples of open-ended questions that can lead to buying signs:

1. "Can you describe the challenges you're currently facing with [relevant topic]?"

By asking this question, you invite customers to articulate their pain points. Their response can provide valuable insights into their needs and create an opportunity for you to offer tailored solutions.

2. "What are your goals or aspirations when it comes to [relevant topic]?"

This question allows customers to share their desires and aspirations. Their answer helps you understand their motivations, allowing you to align your offerings with their goals and create a compelling value proposition.

3. "How would solving [specific problem] impact your day-to-day life or business?"

This question encourages customers to envision the positive outcomes of resolving their challenges. Their response highlights the benefits they seek, helping you tailor your solutions to address their specific needs.

By asking about their past experiences, you gain valuable insights into what they value and what they expect from a product or service. Their feedback helps you position your offerings as superior alternatives, addressing their pain points and concerns.

4. "If you could wave a magic wand and change one thing about your current situation, what would it be?" This question sparks customers' imagination and encourages them to think creatively. Their answer provides a glimpse into their ideal scenario, allowing you to position your offerings as the solution that can make their dreams a reality.

5. "Tell me about your previous experiences with [relevant product or service]. What worked well, and what could have been better?"

This question sparks customers' imagination and encourages them to think creatively. Their answer provides a glimpse into their ideal scenario, allowing you to position your offerings as the solution that can make their dreams a reality.

Chapter 5

Mastering Active Listening: Unlocking Customer Needs and Driving Sales

Welcome, sales enthusiasts, to the world of active listening! In this Chapter, we'll explore the power of listening not only to understand but also to respond effectively. Through active listening, you can uncover valuable buying signs and address customer needs with precision. Remember, the key is to be fully present throughout the conversation, avoiding missed opportunities that could cost you a potential prospect or sale. Let's dive in and discover the art of active listening!

Section 1: Embracing the Dual Purpose of Active Listening

While some people listen solely to respond and others listen merely to understand, active listening requires you to do both. It's a skill that allows you to extract valuable information from conversations, enabling you to identify customer needs and respond with appropriate solutions. Active listening is the secret sauce that propels successful sales interactions.

Section 2: The Buying Signs Hidden in Customer Conversations

During conversations with customers, they often provide subtle clues about their needs and desires. These are known as buying signs. However, it's crucial to slow down and truly listen in order to catch these important signals. Be attentive throughout the entire conversation, not just at the beginning or end. Otherwise, the answers you seek may pass you by, resulting in missed opportunities.

Section 3: Active Listening in Action: Johnny's Encounter

Let's illustrate the power of active listening with an example. Imagine Johnny, a salesperson selling alarm services, meets a friend who shares a story about his 13-year-old daughter. She frequently misses the bus because she oversleeps after her father leaves for work. The conversation may initially seem filled with fluff, but active listening reveals important buying signs.

As Johnny actively listens, he recognizes that his friend leaves the house before his daughter does. So Johnny pitched alarm services with camera access. This would help keep her safe while home alone and allow him to monitor her activities after he leaves for work.

Section 4: Techniques for Active Listening

To master active listening, incorporate these techniques into your sales approach:

Be Fully Present: Give your undivided attention to the customer, focusing on their words, tone, and non-verbal cues. Avoid distractions and demonstrate genuine interest.

Paraphrase and Confirm Understanding: Restate and summarize the customer's statements to ensure you comprehend their needs accurately. Seek clarification when necessary to avoid misinterpretation.

Use Open-Ended Questions: Encourage customers to share more information by asking open-ended questions that require thoughtful responses. This helps uncover additional buying signs and insights.

Practice Empathy: Put yourself in the customer's shoes and understand their perspective. Empathy helps you connect emotionally and build trust, leading to more fruitful conversations.

Palace
NTA
PAR

Section 5: The Rewards of Active Listening

By mastering active listening, you unlock numerous benefits:

Enhanced Customer Relationships: Active listening builds trust and rapport, leading to stronger customer relationships and increased loyalty.

Customized Solutions: By truly understanding customer needs, you can tailor your solutions to address their specific pain points, increasing the likelihood of a successful sale.

Upselling and Cross-Selling Opportunities: Active listening allows you to uncover additional needs and provide relevant recommendations, maximizing your sales potential.

Congratulations, attentive listeners! You have discovered the power of active listening in driving sales success. By listening with intent, catching buying signs, and responding with tailored solutions, you can elevate your sales game to new heights. Embrace the art of active listening, and watch as your customer connections deepen and your sales soar.

Chapter 6

Unveiling the Art of Product Bundling- A Journey into Smart Packaging!

Today, we embark on a thrilling adventure into the world of product bundling. Imagine yourself as a master magician, orchestrating a symphony of perfectly paired items that leave customers spellbound. Get ready to learn how to wow your audience with the captivating power of bundled products.

Section 1: The Magic of Bundling

Picture this: you walk into a store and stumble upon an irresistible offer that seems too good to be true. You're faced with a bundle of products, enticingly packaged together like a treasure trove. This, my friends, is the spell of bundling.

Bundling, in the realm of commerce, is the art of combining multiple products into a single package. It's like bringing together the Avengers to save the day, but in the world of business! This strategic technique allows businesses to maximize their sales potential, enhance customer satisfaction, and even create a touch of magic.

Section 2: Unveiling the Tricks- Examples of Bundling

Now that we've established the allure of bundling, let's dive into two remarkable examples that showcase its spellbinding effect:

Example 1: The Ultimate Home Theater Experience

Imagine being a cinephile who loves movie nights. You stroll into an electronics store and come across a surprising bundle: a high-definition television, a state of- the-art surround sound system, and a collection of blockbuster movies. This bundle is like the Excalibur of home theater experiences. Not only does it offer convenience and value, but it also turns any living room into a cinematic wonderland. Lights, camera, action!

Example 2: The Culinary Adventure Kit

Now, let's venture into the world of cooking. Imagine finding a culinary bundle that includes a chef's knife, a premium cutting board, and a beautifully designed recipe book from a renowned chef. This package is like a chef's best-kept secret, unlocking a world of culinary delights for aspiring gourmets. With this bundle, anyone can transform their kitchen into a Michelin-starred restaurant. Bon appétit!

Section 3: The Magic Formula- Creating Your Own Bundle

Now that you've witnessed the secrets of bundling through these examples, it's time to create your very own magical bundles. Follow these steps to invent a perfect bundle that will bait your customers:

Step 1: Identify Your Target Audience - Understand the needs and desires of your target customers.

Step 2: Select Complementary Products - Choose products that naturally complement each other and enhance the overall customer experience.

Step 3: Determine Pricing and Value - Set a price that offers customers a sense of value while also ensuring profitability for your business.

Step 4: Create Captivating Packaging - Design visually appealing and informative packaging that highlights the benefits of your bundle.

Step 5: Promote and Mesmerize - Utilize effective marketing strategies to promote your bundle and captivate your audience.

Congratulations! You've now unlocked the secrets of product bundling and can harness its powers to captivate your customers. With creativity, strategy, and a touch of showmanship, you can create bundles that leave your competitors spellbound. So, go forth and create your own bundles of wonder. May your sales soar and your customers be forever enticed by the magic you've unleashed!

Remember, the art of bundling is a never-ending journey, full of surprises and innovation. Stay curious, experiment, and keep delighting your customers with your creations.

Chapter 7

The effects of Not Bundling: A Cautionary Tale

While bundling can be a powerful tool in your marketing arsenal, it's essential to understand the potential drawbacks of not utilizing this technique. Here are some cons of forgoing bundling:

Missed Cross-Selling Opportunities: Without bundling, you risk missing out on the chance to cross-sell complementary products. Customers may purchase a single item without realizing that there are other products that could enhance their overall experience. Bundling allows you to showcase the synergies between products and guide customers toward a more comprehensive solution.

Reduced Customer Satisfaction: When customers have to purchase individual items separately, it can be time-consuming and less convenient. This can result in lower customer satisfaction as they may perceive the process as more complex and tedious. Bundling, on the other hand, simplifies the purchasing decision and provides a seamless experience, enhancing customer satisfaction.

Lower Average Order Value: Selling products à la carte can often lead to smaller individual transactions, potentially reducing your average order value. Bundling encourages customers to spend more by offering a perceived value and incentivizing them to purchase multiple items together. By bundling products, you can increase your average order value and boost your overall revenue.

Reduced Upselling and Cross-Selling Opportunities: Without bundling, upselling and cross-selling become more challenging. These techniques rely on presenting additional options and enticing customers to upgrade or add on to their purchase. Bundling allows you to create enticing upgrade packages and seamlessly introduce additional products, increasing the chances of upselling and crossselling.

Impact on Sales Commission: For businesses that rely on commission-based sales, not bundling can affect the potential earnings of your sales team. When selling products individually, the commission earned on each sale may be lower compared to selling a bundled package. Bundling offers an opportunity to increase the overall value of a sale, resulting in higher commissions for your sales team.

Remember, while bundling has its benefits, it's important to strike a balance. Some customers prefer customization and choice, so offering both bundled and à la carte options can cater to a wider range of preferences.

As you journey through the captivating world of product bundling, keep in mind the potential pitfalls of not utilizing this technique. From missed cross-selling opportunities and reduced customer satisfaction to lower average order values and implications for sales commissions, the consequences of forgoing bundling can have a tangible impact on your business.

By embracing the art of bundling, you can maximize customer satisfaction, boost revenue, and create a delightful shopping experience that leaves your customers spellbound. So, let the power of strategic packaging propel your business to new heights!

Chapter 8

Unleashing Sales Confidence: Mastering the Art of Selling with Conviction

Welcome, sales enthusiasts, to the world of unwavering confidence in selling! In this chapter, we'll explore the importance of confidence and how it can elevate your sales performance. Confidence is the driving force that captivates customers, builds trust, and ultimately leads to successful sales. Get ready to unleash your inner sales powerhouse by cultivating confidence and embracing the transformative impact it can have on your sales journey. Let's dive in and embark on this empowering chapter!

Section 1: The Power of Confidence in Sales

Confidence is the secret ingredient that sets successful salespeople apart. When you exude confidence, you radiate credibility, professionalism, and trustworthiness. Your belief in yourself and the product or service you're selling is contagious, attracting customers and instilling in them the confidence to make a purchase.

Section 2: Cultivating Inner Confidence

Building confidence is a journey that requires dedication and self-belief. Here are some key motivational points to help you cultivate inner confidence:

Know Your Product Inside Out:

Take the time to deeply understand your product or service, including its features, benefits, and unique selling points. The more you know, the more confident you will be in conveying its value to customers.

Embrace Continuous Learning:

Stay up-to-date with industry trends, customer preferences, and competitive landscape. Continuously expand your knowledge to remain confident and provide relevant insights to your customers.

Positive Self-Talk:

Replace self-doubt with positive affirmations. Remind yourself of your strengths, accomplishments, and the value you bring to your customers. Embrace a growth mindset and believe in your ability to succeed.

Celebrate Past Successes:

Reflect on your previous sales achievements and celebrate them. Remind yourself of the deals you've closed and the positive impact you've made on your customers. Let these successes fuel your confidence in present and future sales interactions.

Section 3: Body Language and Presentation

Confidence isn't just about what you say—it's also about how you present yourself. Your body language and overall presentation play a vital role in conveying confidence. Consider these tips:

Stand Tall:

Maintain good posture, stand tall, and exude an air of confidence. A straight spine and open body language project assurance and authority.

Maintain Eye Contact:

Establish and maintain strong eye contact with your customers. It demonstrates engagement, trust, and assertiveness. However, be mindful of cultural differences and respect personal boundaries.

Speak with Conviction:

Deliver your sales pitch with clarity, enthusiasm, and conviction. Use confident and assertive language, emphasizing the value and benefits your product or service brings.

Section 4: Building Relationships and Trust

Confidence is not just about selling; it's also about building genuine relationships with your customers. Trust is the foundation of any successful sales interaction.

Consider these relationship-building strategies:

Active Listening:

Demonstrate your confidence by actively listening to your customers. Show genuine interest in their needs and concerns. This helps build rapport, fosters trust, and allows you to tailor your pitch effectively.

Personalize Your Approach:

Understand that each customer is unique. Adapt your sales approach to their individual preferences, needs, and communication styles. This demonstrates your confidence in adapting to different situations and customer profiles.

Provide Solutions:

Confidently offer solutions that address your customers' pain points. Position yourself as a trusted advisor who understands their challenges and has the expertise to provide effective solutions.

Section 5: Embracing Rejection as an Opportunity

In sales, rejection is inevitable. However, a confident salesperson views rejection as an opportunity for growth rather than a personal failure. Embrace rejection with

Chapter 9

The Art of Positioning a SalePersuasive Techniques for Success

Welcome, sales enthusiasts, to the world of strategic sales positioning! In this chapter, we will explore the importance of positioning a sale effectively to maximize your chances of success. We'll delve into persuasive techniques that grab the customer's attention, highlight the value proposition, and create a sense of urgency. Get ready to master the art of positioning and close deals like a pro.

Let's dive in!

Section 1: Understanding the Power of Positioning

Positioning a sale involves presenting your product or service in a compelling and irresistible way. It's about emphasizing its unique features, benefits, and value proposition to create a desire in the customer's mind. By mastering effective positioning techniques, you can captivate your audience and increase your chances of making a sale.

Section 2: Grabbing Attention with a Hook

Begin your sales positioning by capturing the customer's attention with a strong hook. This can be an intriguing question, a compelling statement, or a thought provoking statistic related to their pain points. Here are a few examples:

Question Hook:

"Have you ever wondered how you can increase your productivity by 50% in just one week?"

Statement Hook:

"Introducing our revolutionary new software that will revolutionize the way you manage your finances." Statistic Hook:

"Did you know that 9 out of 10 professionals in your industry have already adopted our cutting-edge solution?"

Section 3: Highlighting the Value Proposition

Once you have the customer's attention, it's time to present the value proposition of your product or service. Clearly communicate the unique features and benefits that set your offering apart from the competition. Focus on how it solves the customer's pain points and improves their lives. Here are a few examples:

Feature-Based Positioning:

"Our new smartphone comes equipped with an industry-leading camera that captures stunning, professional-quality photos."

Benefit-Based Positioning:

"With our fitness program, you'll not only lose weight but also improve your overall well-being, increase energy levels, and boost confidence." Problem-

Solution Positioning:

"Are you tired of manual data entry and the risk of errors? Our automated software streamlines your data management, saving you time and ensuring accuracy."

Section 4: Creating a Sense of Urgency

To motivate customers to take action, it's essential to create a sense of urgency. Highlight limited-time offers, exclusive deals, or scarcity of the product/service to encourage them to make a decision sooner rather than later. Here are a few examples:

Limited-Time Offer:

"Act now and enjoy a 20% discount if you purchase within the next 48 hours." Scarcity Positioning:

"Due to high demand, we have limited stock available. Secure your order today before we run out."

Exclusive Access:

"As a valued customer, you'll gain access to our VIP program, which includes exclusive benefits and personalized support, but only for a limited number of customers."

Section 5: Customizing the Positioning

Remember that effective positioning involves tailoring your approach to each individual customer. Adapt your positioning based on their unique needs, preferences, and pain points. Listen actively and adjust your presentation to address their specific concerns. This personalization will strengthen the customer's connection to your offering.

Congratulations, sales strategists! You have learned the art of positioning a sale to maximize your chances of success. By capturing attention with a compelling hook, highlighting the value proposition, and creating a sense of urgency, you can position your product or service in an irresistible manner. Remember to customize your approach for each customer, listening attentively and addressing their concerns.

Chapter 10

Mastering the Art of Effective Closes- Sealing the Deal with Confidence

Welcome, sales champions, to the world of effective closing techniques! In this tutorial, we'll explore the art of closing sales with finesse, focusing on building trust, understanding customer needs, and timing your close for maximum impact. Say goodbye to the old-school "always be closing" approach and embrace a customer-centric strategy that nurtures relationships and drives successful sales.

Let's dive in!

Section 1: Rethinking the "Always Be Closing" Mindset

Gone are the days of relentless pressure and pushing customers into making hasty decisions. The traditional "always be closing" mantra can sometimes backfire, driving customers away if they feel rushed or manipulated. Instead, adopt a consultative approach that focuses on providing value, building rapport, and empowering customers to make informed decisions.

Section 2: The Power of Timing: Waiting for the Right Moment

One key aspect of effective closing is understanding when to make your move. Rushing into a close before the customer has gathered enough information or is ready to commit can be counterproductive. Exercise patience and gauge the customer's level of interest and understanding before initiating the closing process.

Section 3: Exploring Closing Techniques: Either/Or Closes and Assumptive Closes

Let's delve into two powerful closing techniques that can be used in appropriate situations:

Either/Or Closes: This technique presents the customer with two desirable options, allowing them to choose the one that suits them best. For example:

"Based on what we've discussed, would you prefer Option A with its comprehensive features or Option B with its cost-saving benefits?"

The either/or close empowers the customer to feel in control of their decision while guiding them towards making a choice that aligns with their needs and preferences.

Assumptive Closes: This technique operates under the assumption that the customer has already made the decision to purchase. It reinforces their positive engagement and helps finalize the sale. For example:

"Great! Let's go ahead and schedule the delivery for next week. Which day works best for you?"

The assumptive close assumes that the customer is ready to move forward and simply seeks confirmation. This technique can be effective when you have established a strong rapport and the customer has indicated buying signals.

Section 4: Building Rapport and Addressing Concerns

Before attempting any closing technique, ensure you have built a solid rapport with the customer. Address any remaining concerns or objections they may have, providing reassurance and additional information to instill confidence in their decision-making process. This approach demonstrates your commitment to their satisfaction and builds trust.

Section 5: Closing with Confidence and Respect

When the time is right and you sense that the customer is ready, approach the close with confidence and respect. Use a calm and positive tone, clearly articulating the value and benefits of the purchase. Ask for the sale in a straightforward manner, giving the customer the opportunity to voice any final questions or concerns before making a commitment.

Congratulations, sales champions! You have learned the art of effective closing techniques that prioritize customer trust and confidence. By abandoning the oldschool "always be closing" mindset and embracing consultative selling, you can nurture relationships, provide value, and guide customers towards confident purchasing decisions. Remember to choose your closing techniques wisely, build rapport, address concerns, and time your close for maximum impact. Now, go forth with newfound closing prowess and achieve sales success like never before!

Chapter 11

The Art of Upselling – Maximize Sales Potential

Unleash the power of the upsell! In this chapter, we will explore the art of upselling with energy and enthusiasm. Uncover the secrets to effectively upselling products and services, whether you're catering to a diverse audience of 20-year-olds or individuals of all ages. Learn how to identify opportunities, leverage the psychology of buying signs, and seamlessly guide customers towards making informed purchasing decisions. Get ready to supercharge your sales and elevate your revenue streams.

Section 1: Unleashing the Power of Upselling

Imagine this scenario: you're at your favorite clothing store, browsing through a stylish t-shirt collection. Suddenly, a knowledgeable sales associate approaches you and suggests, "Have you considered pairing that t-shirt with our trendy accessories? They'll take your outfit to a whole new level!" That, my young champions, is the power of upselling. Upselling is the art of persuading customers to upgrade their purchase or add complementary items that enhance their overall experience. It's like acquiring a lightsaber to become a true style Jedi!

Section 2: Unveiling the Master Moves: Examples of Upselling

Let's unveil three thrilling examples that will help you grasp the incredible potential of upselling in your sales endeavors:

Example 1: The Fashion Forward Ensemble

Imagine you're shopping online for a stylish pair of jeans. As you're about to complete your purchase, a clever pop-up appears, suggesting, "Complete your look with a matching jacket and a pair of trendy sneakers!" This upsell transforms your outfit from casual to fashion-forward, allowing you to make a style statement wherever you go. Embrace your individuality, young trendsetters!

Example 2: The Epic Concert Experience

Picture yourself buying tickets to see your favorite band perform live. Just before checkout, a savvy ticketing platform recommends, "Upgrade to VIP tickets for exclusive access to the pre-show party and a meet-and-greet with the band!" This upsell elevates your concert experience from great to absolutely unforgettable, making you feel like a true rock star. Rock on, young music enthusiasts!

Example 3: The Adventure Travel Package

Now, let's venture into the realm of travel. You're planning a trip to a dream destination and booking your flight online. The travel website entices you, saying, "Enhance your journey with a travel package that includes hotel accommodations, sightseeing tours, and a local guide!" This upsell transforms your vacation into an immersive adventure, ensuring you make the most of every moment. Wanderlust awaits, young explorers!

Section 3: Mastering Your Upselling Skills

Now that you've witnessed the impressive effects of upselling, it's time to master your own upselling skills. Here are three key steps to become an upselling Jedi:

Understand Your Audience: Get to know your target market—their preferences, aspirations, and desires. Tailor your upselling techniques to their specific interests and showcase how your recommendations align with their lifestyle.

Highlight Added Value: Emphasize the unique benefits and features of the upgraded product or additional items. Show how they enhance the overall experience, provide convenience, or offer an extra touch of luxury or enjoyment.

Create a Personalized Journey: Make tailored recommendations based on the customer's initial purchase or interests. Help them envision how the upsell will complement and enhance their experience, allowing them to get the most out of their purchase.

Congratulations, sales warriors! You have unlocked the secrets of upselling and are now poised to dominate the sales arena. Remember, upselling is about understanding your audience, showcasing added value, and creating personalized journeys. So, ignite your selling powers, embrace your inner upselling Jedi, and watch your sales skyrocket to new heights!

Section 3: The Art of Active Listening

Asking the right questions is only half the battle. The other half is mastering the art of active listening. Pay close attention to your customers' responses, focus on their words, and seek to understand their underlying needs and motivations. Engage in meaningful dialogue, ask follow-up questions, and show genuine interest in their responses. This will create a trusting and collaborative environment that encourages customers to open up further.

Congratulations, budding sales experts! You now possess the knowledge and skills to probe effectively and ask the right questions. Remember, open-ended questions are your allies in uncovering customer needs and identifying buying signals. By practicing active listening and using these probing techniques, you can build stronger connections with your customers and guide them towards making confident purchasing decisions. So, embrace the art of probing, ask thoughtful questions, and unlock the secrets to successful sales interactions!

Chapter 12

Mastering the Art of Rebuttals-Overcoming Objections to Boost Sales

Welcome, sales warriors, to the world of rebuttals! In this Chapter, we'll explore the power of overcoming objections and how effective rebuttals can transform a potential setback into a sales opportunity. Remember, the sale doesn't truly begin until the customer presents objections. It is in those moments that skilled salespeople shine, demonstrating their ability to address concerns, build trust, and ultimately increase sales. Let's dive in and discover the art of rebuttals!

Section 1: Embracing Objections as Opportunities

Objections are not roadblocks; they are stepping stones on the path to a successful sale. Rather than viewing objections negatively, perceive them as an invitation to engage in a deeper conversation with the customer. Embrace objections as opportunities to showcase your expertise, understanding, and commitment to meeting their needs.

Section 2: The Power of Effective Rebuttal

Rebuttal is the art of providing persuasive responses to overcome objections and address customer concerns. It involves active listening, empathy, and providing relevant information to instill confidence in the customer. By mastering the art of effective rebuttal, you can transform objections into reasons to move forward with the sale.

Section 3: Strategies for Successful Rebuttal

Here are some strategies to help you navigate objections and successfully close the sale:

Active Listening and Empathy:

Take the time to truly listen to the customer's objection and understand their perspective. Empathize with their concerns and demonstrate genuine care for their needs. This builds trust and allows you to respond effectively.

Clarify and Reiterate:

Restate the objection to ensure you fully understand the customer's concern. This demonstrates that you value their input and are committed to addressing it appropriately. It also allows the customer to feel heard and understood.

Provide Value and Solutions:

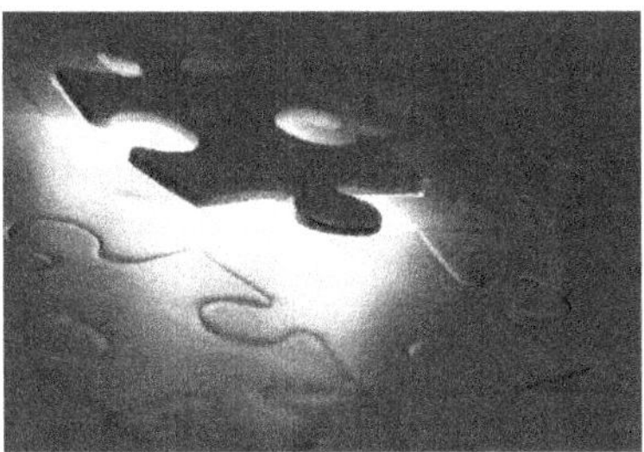

Address the objection by highlighting the value and benefits of your product or service. Focus on the specific features that directly address the customer's concerns. Offer solutions and alternatives that showcase how your offering can meet their needs.

Social Proof and Testimonials:

Share success stories and testimonials from satisfied customers who have had similar objections. By providing social proof, you instill confidence in the customer and alleviate their concerns, showing them that others have experienced positive outcomes.

Ask Thought-Provoking Questions:

Engage the customer in a thoughtprovoking dialogue to help them reconsider their objection. Ask questions that challenge their assumptions or highlight additional benefits they may not have considered.

This encourages them to think more deeply about their concerns.

Section 4: Adapting and Improving

Remember, each objection is an opportunity to learn and refine your sales approach. Pay attention to the objections you encounter most frequently and develop rebuttals specific to those concerns. Continually refine your rebuttal techniques based on customer feedback, industry trends, and your own experiences.

Section 5: Persistence and Resilience

In the face of objections, stay persistent and resilient. Understand that objections are a natural part of the sales process and not a personal rejection. Approach objections with professionalism and a positive attitude. Adapt your rebuttals as needed, always striving to find the best solution for your customers.

You have now unlocked the secrets of effective rebuttals and overcoming objections. By viewing objections as opportunities and mastering the art of persuasive response, you can increase sales, build stronger relationships, and earn the trust of your customers. Remember, the true mark of a skilled salesperson lies in their ability to navigate objections with confidence and provide compelling solutions. Now, go forth armed with your newfound rebuttal prowess and watch your sales soar to new heights.

Conclusion:

Congratulations, aspiring sales Masters! By embarking on this journey of mastering sales excellence, you have tapped into a wellspring of untapped potential that lies within you. You now possess the key to unlock previously closed doors, and the power to achieve sales greatness like never before.

Remember, success in sales is not always about what you do, but how you do it. It's about harnessing the power of your unique personality, skills, and techniques to leave an indelible mark on every customer interaction. It's about becoming a sales goat—a true master of your craft.

As you go forth, armed with newfound knowledge, let your passion blaze like a wildfire, your energy radiate like a shining star, and your enthusiasm ignite the hearts of every customer you encounter. Embrace the art of persuasion, knowing that it is your genuine connection, unwavering belief, and unwavering dedication that will set you apart from the rest.

In this competitive world of sales, remember that every setback is an opportunity for a comeback, every rejection is a chance to refine your approach, and every challenge is a stepping stone toward greatness. Keep pushing boundaries, learning, adapting, and growing.

Believe in yourself, for you possess the power to create lasting impressions, forge meaningful relationships, and achieve extraordinary sales results. Embrace the role of a sales Master, leading the herd with unwavering confidence, unwavering determination, and unwavering excellence. Remember, it's not just about making sales—it's about transforming lives, meeting needs, and creating meaningful connections. The journey to sales greatness begins now. Embrace it. Own it. And let your passion roar!

You are a Sales Master, and the world is yours for the taking! Now that you have mastered the art of sales it is important to keep sharpening your iron and practicing your craft. Visit our YouTube and Instagram pages today and start your transformational journey toward financial freedom and a better way of life. Remember, success in sales is not just about what you do—it's about how you do it.

Together, let's master the art of sales, make power moves in the business world, and create a life of abundance and fulfillment. Click that subscribe button on YouTube and hit the follow button on Instagram to join our community of sales champions. Get ready to make your mark, leave a lasting legacy, and embrace a life of limitless possibilities. Your journey to sales mastery begins now. Visit our

YouTube and Instagram pages and let's make power moves together!

Power_moves1   Power_Movesig

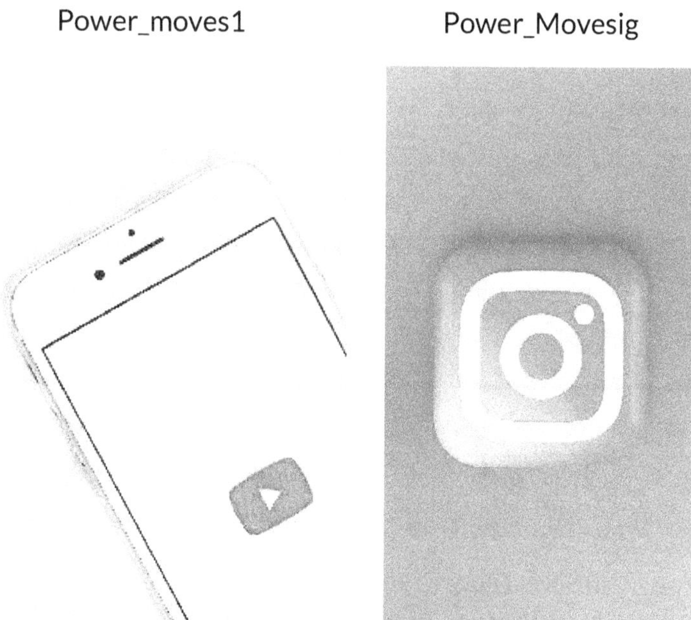

Dedication:

To God my loving wife and three incredible children,

This book is dedicated to each of you, my pillars of strength, my unwavering support, and the driving force behind my journey. Without your love, encouragement, and belief in me, this endeavor would not have been possible.

To my beloved wife, you are my rock, my confidante, and my biggest cheerleader. Your unwavering belief in my dreams has fueled my determination to overcome challenges and reach for the stars. Your unconditional love has been the guiding light that illuminates my path, inspiring me to push beyond my limits and strive for greatness.

To my precious children, you are my inspiration, my motivation, and the reason I strive to be the best version of myself. Watching you grow, learn, and embrace life's adventures fills my heart with immeasurable joy. Your laughter, your hugs, and your unwavering faith in me give me the strength to persevere even in the face of adversity.

Together, as a family, we have shared the highs and lows, the triumphs and tribulations. You have witnessed my journey firsthand, celebrated my successes, and stood by me during moments of doubt. Your unwavering support and understanding have been the fuel that propels me forward, reminding me that anything is possible with love and determination.

This book serves as a testament to the profound impact you have had on my life. It is a symbol of gratitude for the sacrifices you have made, the late nights you have endured, and the unwavering belief you have bestowed upon me. You have been my pillars of strength, my sounding board, and my constant source of love and inspiration.

Thank you for being the wind beneath my wings, for believing in me when I doubted myself, and for reminding me that together, we can conquer any challenge that comes our way. I am forever grateful to have you by my side, and I cherish every moment we have together.

With all my Love,

Demario Cromity